# Catches and Glees

## of the Eighteenth Century

SELECTED BY
B. H. BRONSON
from
APOLLONIAN HARMONY
(ca. 1790)

UNIVERSITY OF CALIFORNIA PRESS
BERKELEY AND LOS ANGELES 1955

SECOND PRINTING, REVISED

UNIVERSITY OF CALIFORNIA PRESS
BERKELEY AND LOS ANGELES, CALIFORNIA
CAMBRIDGE UNIVERSITY PRESS
LONDON, ENGLAND

COPYRIGHT, 1955, BY
THE REGENTS OF THE UNIVERSITY OF CALIFORNIA

# Apollonian Harmony:

*a Collection of scarce & celebrated*
GLEES CATCHES, MADRIGALS,
CANZONETTS, ROUNDS, & CANONS.
*Antient & Modern with some Originals*
Composed by
*Aldrich, Arne, Atterbury, Battishall, Boyce,
Brewer, Dibdin, Eccles, Est, Giardini, Green
Hundel, Harrington, Hayes, Hook, Morley
Nares, Purcell, Ravenscroft, Travers, Webbe*
and other eminent Masters;
*most of which are sung at the Noblemens*
CATCH-CLUB, THEATRES, & PUBLIC-GARDENS
*The Words consistent with Female Delicacy*

| VOL. 2 | Be Merry and Wise | Pr. 4 |

LONDON.
Printed at Button Whitaker's, Music Warehouse 75 St Pauls Church Y$^d$
where may be had

|  | s | d |
|---|---|---|
| The Flights of Fancy a Collection of Glees by M$^r$ Linley | 10 | 6 |
| The Ladies Catch book a Coll$^n$ of Catches Canons & Glees by Webb | 5 | 0 |
| A Fourth Book of Catches Canons & Glees by Webb | 10 | 6 |
| Six English Canzonets for 2, & 3. Voices by Hook Op: 18$^{th}$ | 2 | 6 |
| Catches Glees & Canons for 3. 4. 5. & 6. Voices by D$^r$ Hayes | 10 | 6 |

To
RANDALL THOMPSON,
"Dog at a Catch"

*Ladies and Gentlemen:*

*The Eighteenth Century, as you well know, was noteworthy for its social spirit. In this respect, it stands conspicuously apart from its predecessor and successor. It had turned away from the passionate religious fervor of the Seventeenth Century, and it was in turn to be supplanted by the introspective mood of the Romantic Age. Its most characteristic forms of artistic expression are concerned with Man in his social environment. In architecture, it built admirable dwelling houses, not lofty churches; in its hands the utilitarian arts and crafts rose to a level seldom surpassed. Its sculptors modeled statues and busts of actual men and women; its painters were preëminent in contemporary portraiture; its authors attained the foremost rank in history, biography, and the novel.*

*In music, it was natural that such an age should find congenial those forms especially that were sociable and popular: song, sacred or secular, and the rhythms of the dance. The nightly concerts of the Pleasure Gardens gave scope for a vast outpouring of songs of the lighter sort; and the ballad operas were, essentially, appealing anthologies of popular airs, both new and old. In that "clubbable" age, clubs were established whose sole purpose was to foster convivial singing. Of this kind were The Noblemen's and Gentlemen's Catch Club (founded in 1761 and still in existence); the Concentores Sodales; the Glee Club; and—oldest of all surviving musical societies—the Hibernian Catch Club, established about 1680. These organizations sponsored annual prizes for the best compositions in the forms of catch and glee; and, between them, must have been responsible for the publication of well over a hundred volumes of such pieces.*

*Many of the best catches display great ingenuity in so disposing and interweaving the words as to produce a surprising and ludicrous effect when the parts are sung together; but* double entendre *is not indispensable, and mimetic effects of various kinds are welcomed:—snoring, sneezing, yawning, laughing; vocal imitation of bells, and the combining of street cries. These forms were structurally varieties of the canon or round. They were by no means new; but they attained a renewed and wide-spread popularity in the days of Johnson and Boswell. The glee is a relatively homophonic sort of choral song, unaccompanied, blocked out in rather short sections, and easier to follow than the madrigal. It is from a single collection of such pieces, put together apparently in the last decade of the century and published in six undated volumes, that all the songs here reproduced have been chosen.*

*It only remains, in an age wherein the noise of motors and machines grows more and more strident, to urge the convivially minded to put this little book to its right use:*

> Now we are met let mirth abound
> And let the catch and toast go round!

*Such a consummation, as it was his only aim, would be the happiest reward of the compiler, who begs to subscribe himself*

*Yours in all duty and obedience,*
BERTRAND BRONSON

*Berkeley, California*
*April, 1955*

---

The first printing of this collection appeared in 1939, prompted by the timely stimulus and practical counsel of him to whom the revised edition is now dedicated.

# CONTENTS

**CATCHES AND CANONS**

| | |
|---|---|
| Ars longa, vita brevis, 13 | Hayes |
| Buz, quoth the blue Flie, 9 | Arne |
| Chairs to Mend, 25 | Hayes |
| Come follow me, 32 | Bates |
| Come, my boys, let's sing a Catch, 6 | Carter |
| Cuckow, 3 | Anon |
| Curs'd be the Wretch, 8 | Carey |
| Ding dong boam Bell, 21 | Taylor |
| Give me the sweet Delights of Love, 17 | Harrington |
| Half an Hour past twelve o'clock, 23 | Marella |
| Here Innocence and Beauty lies, 30 | Travers |
| Here's a Health to all them, 33 | Anon |
| How happy are we now the Wind is abaft, 28 | Berg |
| I cannot sing this Catch, 3 | Harrington |
| If Eve in her Innocence, 16 | Webbe |
| If neither Brass nor Marble, 13 | Hayes |
| I've lost my Mistress, 19 | Greene |
| Let us be merry in our old Cloaths, 27 | Gregory |
| Mister Speaker tho' 'tis late, 26 | Baildon |
| Now we are met let mirth abound, 1 | Webbe |
| Oh ever against eating Cares, 29 | Hayes |
| Pretty Maidens, 20 | Atterbury |
| Says Damon to Chloe, 18 | Webbe |
| See, Bob, see, the Play is done, 10 | Arne |
| Sir you are a comical Fellow, 12 | Bates |
| So peaceful rests, 30 | Greene |
| Sure Women and Wine, 22 | Hayes |

| | |
|---|---|
| Sweep, Chimney Sweep, 4 | Arne |
| Sweet enslaver, can you tell, 20 | Atterbury |
| Tis hum drum, 21 | Harrington |
| Tis thus and thus, 31 | Boyce |
| Two Lawyers when a knotty Cause, 14 | Cuzens |
| Ut, Re, Mi, Fa, Sol, La, 2 | Anon |
| Uxor mea, 5 | Anon |
| Viva Londra!, 24 | Cocchi |
| White Sand and gray Sand, 21 | Anon |
| Wilt thou lend me thy Mare, 27 | Nares |
| Wou'd you sing a Catch with Pleasure, 1 | Anon |
| Yah—Atchee—Oh—Ha, 9 | Anon |
| Ye Heav'ns, if Innocence, 22 | Baildon |
| You beat your Pate, 15 | Hayes |

GLEES (CANZONETS, BACCHANALS, AND ELEGIES)

| | |
|---|---|
| A bumper of good Liquor, 36 | Linley |
| All in the Downs, 47 | Anon |
| Blow blow thou Winter's Wind, 54 | Arne |
| Colla bottiglia in mano, 45 | Cocchi |
| Come live with me, 48 | Webbe |
| Come Shepherds (Elegy on the Death of Mr. Shenstone), 59 | Arne |
| How sleep the Brave, 63 | Ireland |
| Hush to peace, each ruder Wind, 55 | Arne |
| Sigh no more, Ladies, 52 | Arne |
| This Bottle's the Sun of our Table, 34 | Linley |
| Time has not thin'd my flowing Hair, 38 | Jackson |
| To fair Fidele's grassy Tomb, 58 | Arne |
| Which is the properest day to drink, 42 | Arne |

## CATCH

See what you want or please to buy,
Cure, a Cure for the Tooth-ach, a Drop for your
all. Here's London in lit-tle. Here's Pa- -ris in
Half a Crown, for Half a Crown, for

See what you want or please to buy.
Eye, a Drop, a Drop for your Eye.
Town; Here's Paris, here's Pa - ris in Town. The
Half a Crown, for Half a Crown.

ROUND.

1. Uxor me - a, Uxor polla,
2. O fi frangat fu - a colla,.
3. Pol - la col - la col - la pol - la.

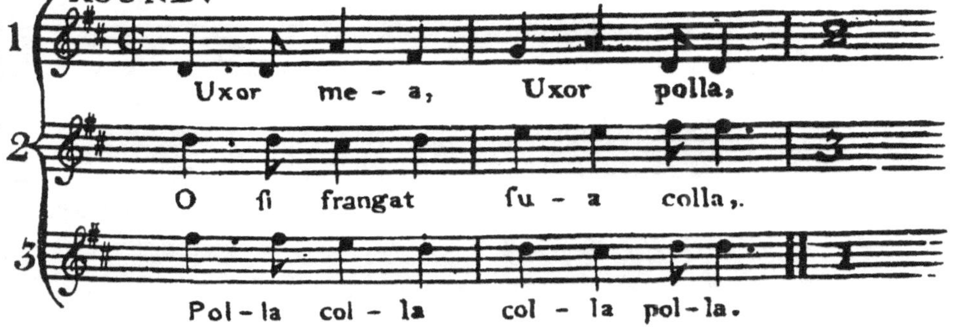

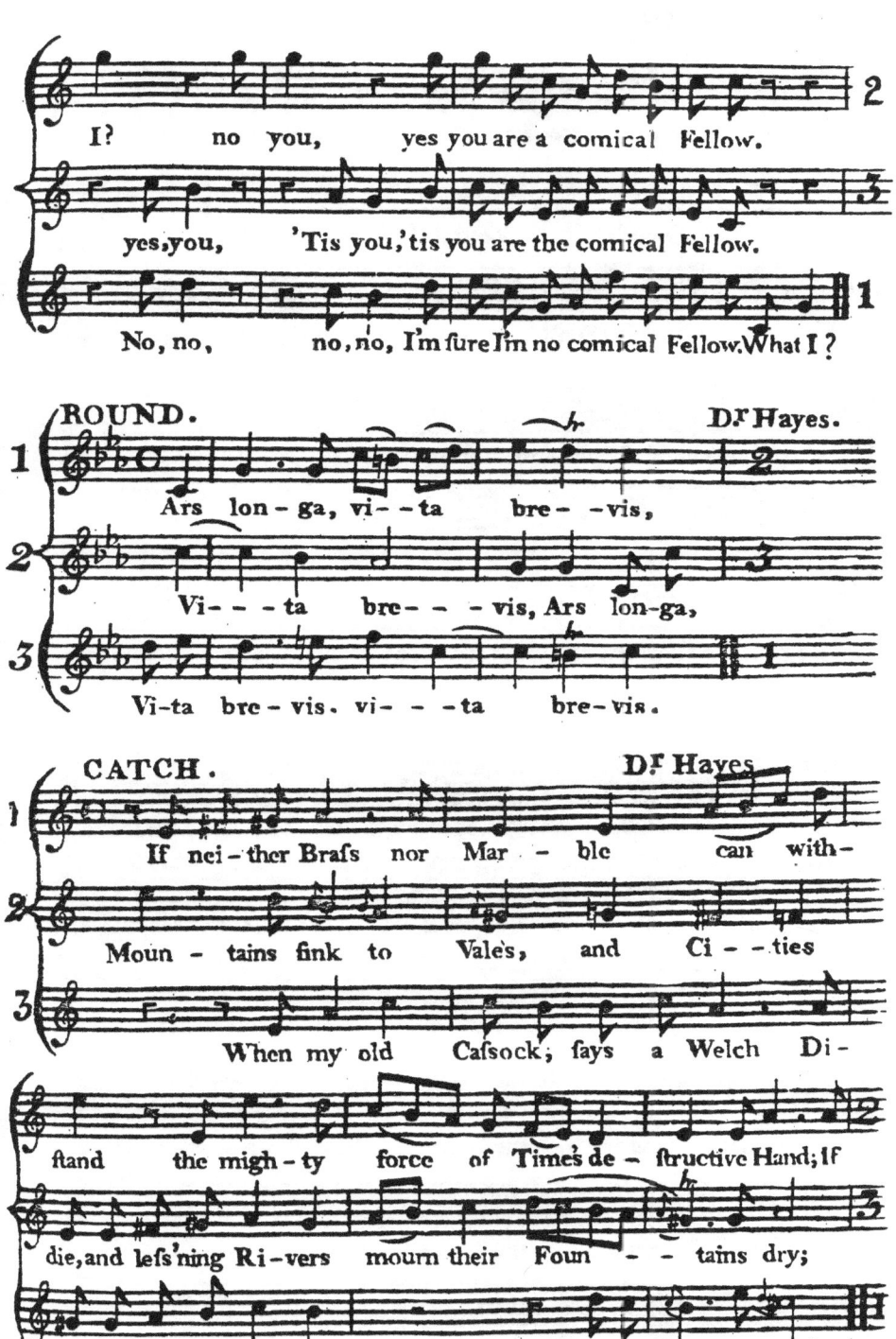

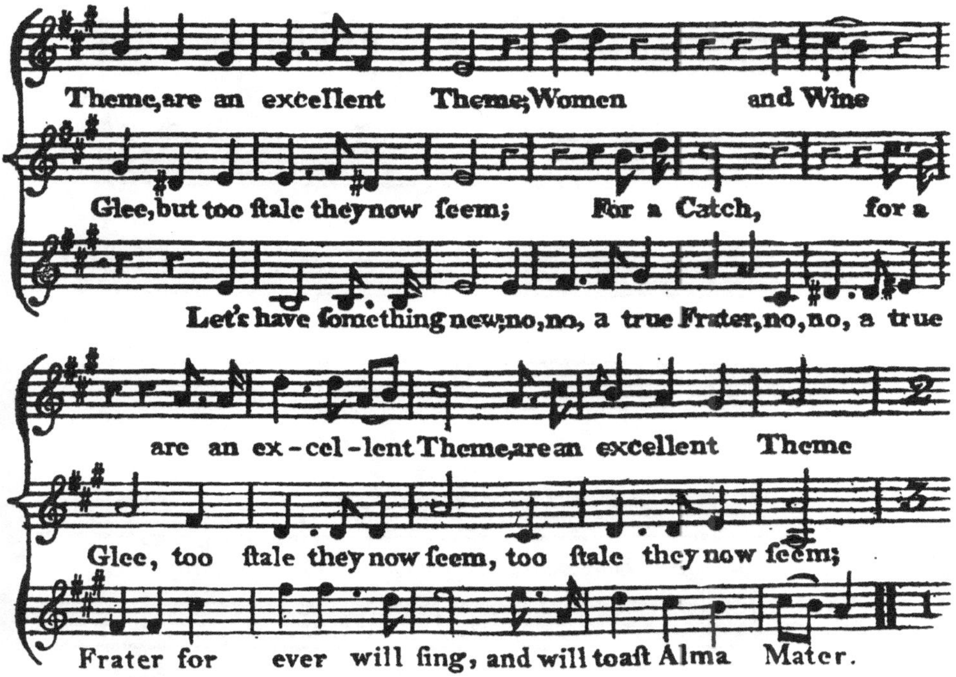

Theme, are an excellent Theme; Women and Wine
Glee, but too stale they now seem; For a Catch, for a
Let's have something new; no, no, a true Frater, no, no, a true
are an ex-cel-lent Theme, are an excellent Theme
Glee, too stale they now seem, too stale they now seem;
Frater for ever will sing, and will toast Alma Mater.

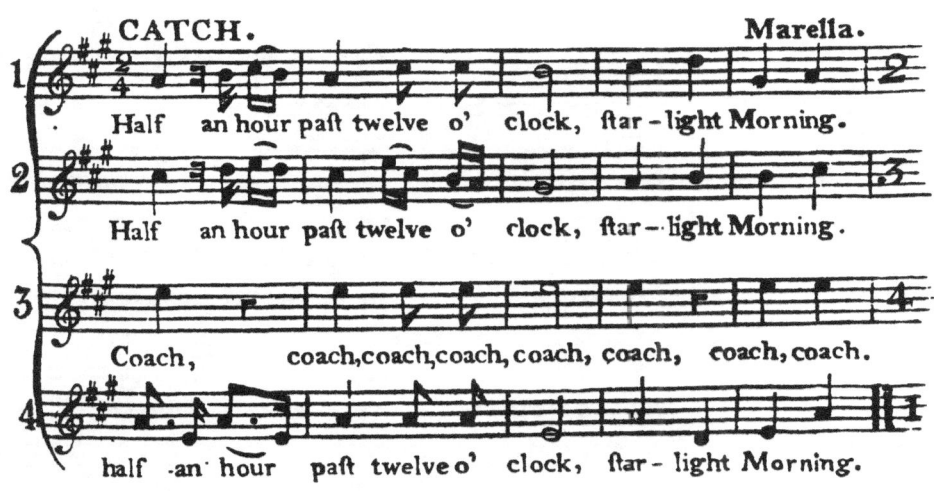

CATCH. Marella.

1. Half an hour past twelve o' clock, star-light Morning.

2. Half an hour past twelve o' clock, star-light Morning.

3. Coach, coach, coach, coach, coach, coach, coach, coach.

4. half an hour past twelve o' clock, star-light Morning.

CATCH E. Gregory.

CATCH. Dr Nares.

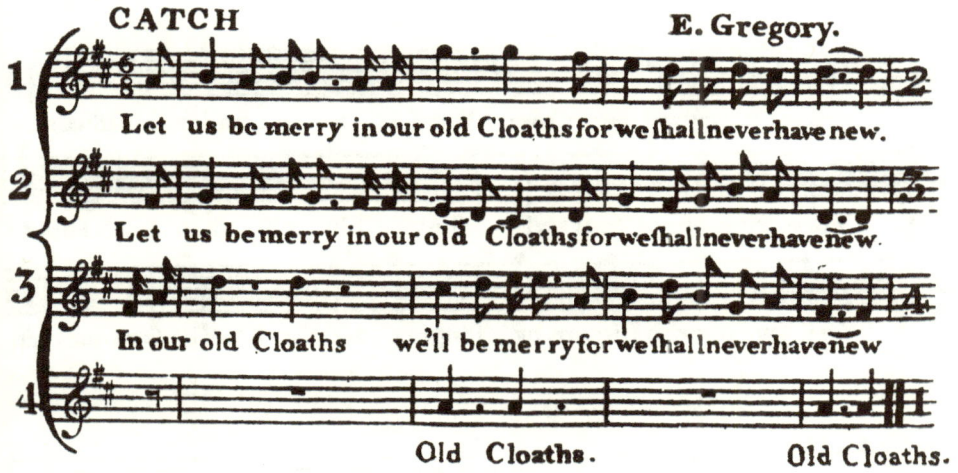

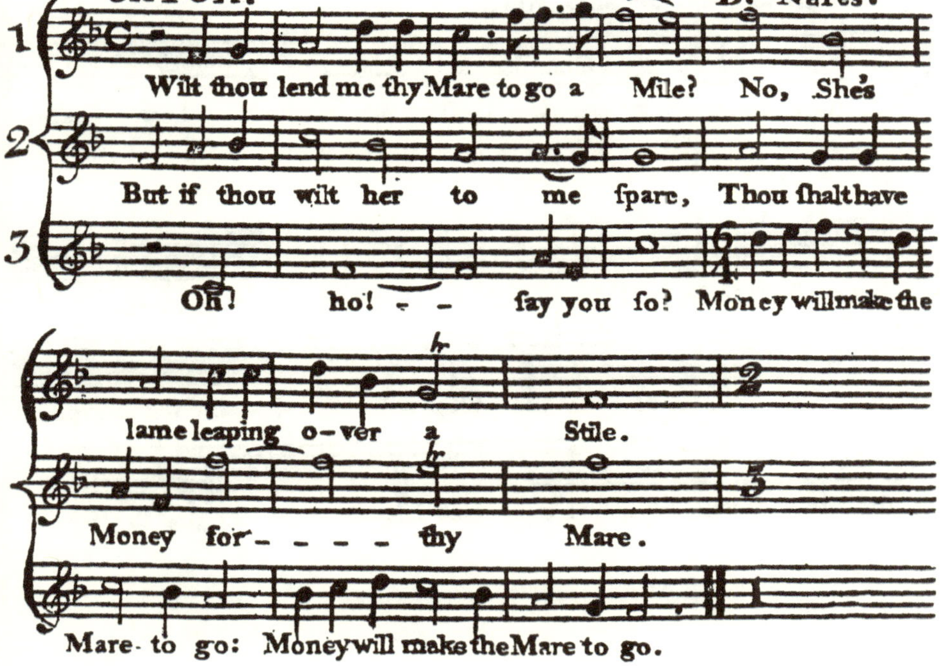

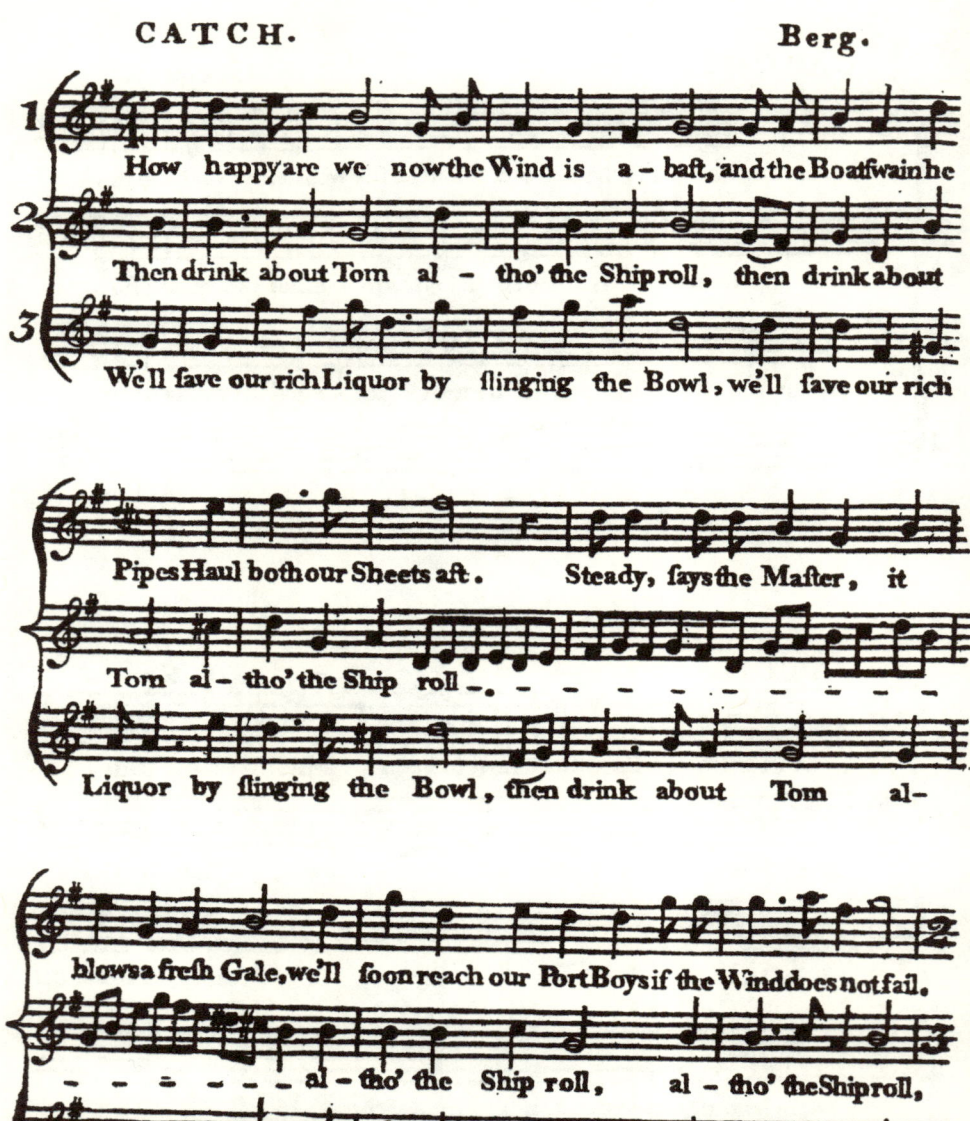

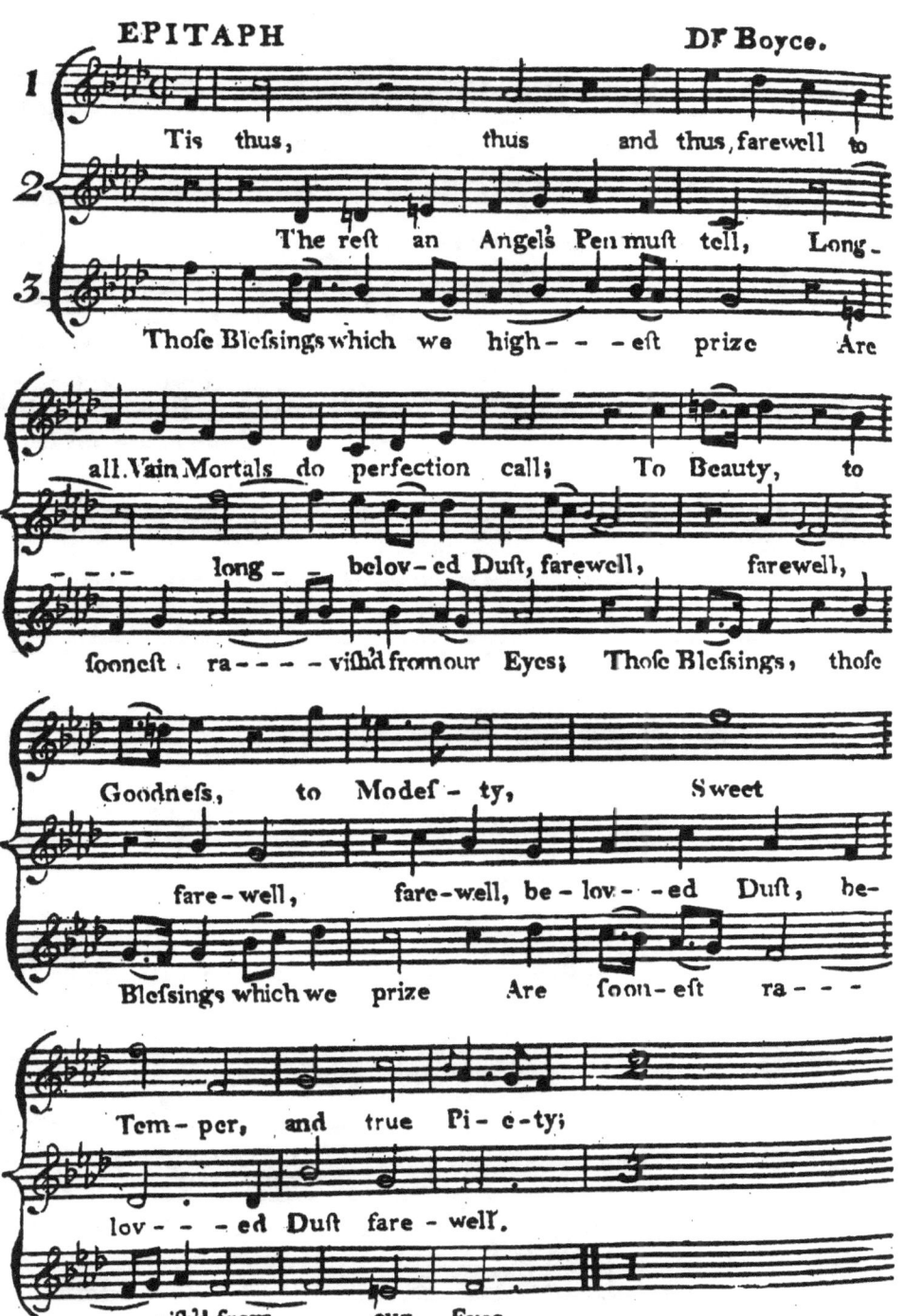

[33]

[40]

Sing no more Ditties, sing no more
Of Dumps so dull and heavy;
The Frauds of Men were ever so
Since Summer first was leafy:
Then sigh not so, but let them go,
And be you blithe and merry,
Converting all your Notes of Woe
Into hey down derry.

The Redbreast oft at ev'ning Hours  
Shall kindly lend his little aid,  
With hoary Moss and gather'd Flow'rs,  
To deck the Ground where thou art laid.

When howling Winds, and beating Rain  
In Tempest shake the Sylvan Cell,  
Or midst the Chace on ev'ry Plain  
The tender thought on thee shall dwell

Each lonely Scene shall thee restore,  
For thee the tear be duly shed;  
Belov'd till Life cou'd charm no more;  
And mourn'd 'till Pity's self be dead.

[62]

www.ingramcontent.com/pod-product-compliance
Lightning Source LLC
Chambersburg PA
CBHW021716230426
43668CB00008B/856